I.M.P.A.C.T.

Embracing the Power of Your Story

by Joseph C. Richardson, Ph.D., PMP

Printed in the United States of America

Published by:
Horned Horse Publishing

Cover Art by Sara Marie E.B.

ISBN: 979-8-9908914-3-2

I dedicate this book to my wonderful wife, Felicia, and our
fantastic children, Ryan, Lyndsay, and Nathan.

"I am the vine; you are the branches.
If you remain in me and I in you, you will bear much fruit;
apart from me you can do nothing"
(John 15:5, NIV).

I.M.P.A.C.T.

Table of Contents

Introduction

"I have no gift to bring,
Pa rum pumpumpum,
That's fit to give our King."
—*"The Little Drummer Boy" by Katherine Kennicott Davis*

I am thrilled to invite you on the journey of a guy whose initial outlook on life was like the lyrics from "The Little Drummer Boy" that you just read. This was a person who initially thought he had nothing of true value to add to this world and saw no way his story would ever be impactful to anyone. His journey started out in the Henry Horner projects on the West Side of Chicago. As a teenager, he enlisted in the U.S. Air Force and stumbled onto an unconventional path that a few years later would find him as the #1 cadet in rank and position at the prestigious U.S. Air Force Academy. In this book, you'll get a peek at his path from nearly failing out of college to receiving two master's degrees and a Ph.D. from a renowned university, which led to being a college instructor at the technical college, undergraduate, and graduate degree levels. You'll learn about his journey from a 26.5-year career in the military to being the Vice President of Student Affairs at Valencia College in Orlando, one of the largest state colleges in America. This guy was me, and this was my path—the winding road that led me to a career as an entrepreneur, author, and speaker. The story of my life is continuing to be written, but it is my hope and prayer that as you read what has transpired thus far, you will be filled with hope, faith, and amazement for how God can work through and use a rather ordinary person in a profound and significant way.

My faith in God and my Christian worldview will be evident throughout this book. I'll use biblical passages and stories often, not to isolate others who may look at life differently, but as a way of ensuring I stay genuine and authentic to who I am. I can tell my story no other way. As I reflect on the history of my life, I'm reminded that my journey is essentially HIS-story, and that God has had His fingerprints on every aspect of my existence.

As I share my story, I invite you to consider the value of your life journey as well. What is your story? Have you ever shared it with anyone? Are you aware that your story, regardless of the good, the bad, or the ugly it contains, is a powerful tool to help you positively impact the lives of others? There are people you pass by, wave at, have a casual conversation with, or work with who have amazing stories filled with inspiration that you have no idea about.

My main goal in writing this book is to give you a framework for sharing your own story in a way that adds value to others' lives. I want to encourage you to embrace the totality of your past and realize there are no insignificant events. I want to challenge you to understand that somebody, somewhere, possibly at this very moment, needs to hear about the challenges you've faced, the failures you've endured, the victories that you have snatched from the jaws of defeat, and the powerful lessons you've learned along the way.

Through the parts of my story that I tell in each chapter of this book, I'll introduce you to and demonstrate the "I.M.P.A.C.T." model for telling your own story. The IMPACT model will help you define your life's key moments and share the lessons you've learned from them with others. In short, this model invites you to consider the following:

Inspiration: Understand that your inspiration comes from your foundations.

Moments: Highlight the moments in your life that put you on the path to personal growth.

Purpose: Find what drives you and adds satisfaction to your life.

Adversity: Recognize how your challenges drove necessary course corrections.

Connection: Celebrate and prioritize the people who supported you and shaped your life.

Transformation: Embrace your growth and your contributions to life's big picture.

As I mentioned earlier, part of my journey consisted of serving in the military, specifically as a navigator of surveillance/reconnaissance and command/control aircraft. My role on the flight crew was to set the plane's course so the pilot knew which direction to go. Before aviators went out to the actual plane to fly a mission, we would often attend simulator training, which allowed us to practice the techniques and procedures we would use on the flight. That way, when we actually flew the mission, there was a degree of familiarity we could embrace. Both in the simulators and on the actual aircraft, we would stay on course by using "waypoints" set at particular geographic locations or reference points along our route.

Similarly, each part of the I.M.P.A.C.T. acronym can serve as a "waypoint" to guide you down the path of sharing your story. You don't have to use every element of the acronym every time you tell someone your story. Depending on who you're talking to or the time you have, you may just want to use one or two parts. However, to help you embrace the full power of your life experiences, I hope you'll eventually explore every part of the I.M.P.A.C.T. model. Eventually, as you become more comfortable using the I.M.P.A.C.T. model, you'll be able to use your story to its greatest potential to positively influence the world around you. In the chapters ahead, as I use the I.M.P.A.C.T. framework to tell my story, I hope you'll gain some insight from stopping at my life's waypoints that will prepare you to share your own story with others.

By the time you finish this book, I hope you will also know, without a doubt, that your story is valuable. In the book of Matthew, Chapter 9, verses 35-38 (NKJV), it says:

> *Then Jesus went about all the cities and villages, teaching in their synagogues, preaching the gospel of the kingdom, and healing every sickness and every disease among the people. But when He saw the multitudes, He was moved with compassion for them, because they were weary and scattered, like sheep having no shepherd. Then He said to His disciples, "The harvest truly is plentiful, but the laborers are few. Therefore pray the Lord of the harvest to send out laborers into His harvest."*

I recently had a conversation with my brother Maurice (you'll read more about him later) about this passage of scripture. We talked about how there are people in our circle who still walk around feeling weary and scattered like the people described in these verses. We talked about the need for more "laborers" who can help provide the support needed during the times we live in today. This book is an urgent call for laborers. It's a call for everyone to become a participant in adding value to others' lives. It's a call for YOU to use the power of YOUR story to help and support others in a way that no one else can.

Maurice and I also had a heartfelt conversation about how the story of Jesus's life and ministry is not told from the perspective of just one of His disciples. We could've had only the story of His life as described by Matthew or Mark, or Luke, or John. Why is the story of His life told by

Matthew and Mark and Luke and John? It's because God revealed Himself uniquely to each of them, and each of their accounts of His life and ministry is different based on how they experienced Him. It works the same way with our lives. I believe that your spiritual experience is uniquely different from that of any other person on this planet, and people will be touched by hearing about your unique experiences in life differently than they will be touched by mine. There are people you can reach and help in ways that the greatest preachers and teachers on earth cannot.

The people in your sphere of influence need to hear from you. Regardless of the medium of communication you use, your power to uplift the people around you is unlike any other person's and is unique only to you. And if you don't tell your story yourself, the valuable lessons others can learn from it may be missed. Responding to the message of this book by taking action and becoming a steward of the story you've been given will give you the opportunity to be an encouragement and inspiration to those around you.

My hope is to encourage you and show you through my life story that God can and will use anybody who surrenders to His will. We all have a story to tell, and for every story there is to be told, there are people somewhere who need to hear it. You may not see value or significance in your journey, but that doesn't equate to the absence of value and significance. Your background, the kind of family or situation you were born into, certainly matters, but it isn't your complete story. What matters is who God is and how willing you are to go on the adventure He has planned for you to create a life of impact.

I often think of myself as God's little bag of rocks. That sounds somewhat self-deprecating until you read the story of David and Goliath in 1 Samuel 17:48-49 (NIV):

> *As the Philistine moved closer to attack him, David ran quickly toward the battle line to meet him. Reaching into his bag and taking out a stone, he slung it and struck the Philistine on the forehead. The stone sank into his forehead, and he fell facedown on the ground.*

Those small, smooth stones turned into giant-slayers when they were in the hands of God's servant and energized by His power. As I think of David, I'm again reminded of how much I've always identified with"The Little Drummer Boy." Just like the boy in the song, I felt I had no gifts to bring that were fit to give the King. Fortunately for me, the King had his own set of gifts, which He used to energize and inspire me to live a life that glorifies His name and contributes to the advancement of His kingdom.

I believe each person on this planet is a treasure chest, and that if we simply take the time to explore what's on the inside, we will discover the treasures of immeasurable value that each person contains. This belief I have reminds me of the verse in the Bible that says:

> *"Jesus also did many other things. If every one of them were written down, I suppose the world wouldn't have enough room for the books that would be written"* (John 21:25, GWT).

This verse moves me to think of all the billions of lives that have existed and the amazing stories that were a part of those lives. I'm convinced that for every story in the Bible that was recorded, there are many more testimonies that were not recorded that could have been a similar source of guidance, encouragement, and inspiration. Without sounding blasphemous, I also believe that if God wanted to, He could use the stories of people on the planet right now to make an equally inspiring edition of the Bible today. In fact, 2 Corinthians 3:2-3 (NIV) says that:

> *You yourselves are our letter, written on our hearts, known and read by everyone. You show that you are a letter from Christ, the result of our ministry, written not with ink but with the Spirit of the living God, not on tablets of stone but on tablets of human hearts.*

According to this verse, each of us represents a letter, a book, a story that needs to be told. My quest to be the best steward of the story I've been given is what inspired me to write this book and share my story. So, buckle up, fasten your seatbelts tight, and let's go on this journey together.

Chapter 1

Inspiration:
The Powerful Effect of Family

"In every conceivable manner, the family is the link to our past, the bridge to our future." – Alex Haley

My values are God, family, and then everything else. I received this precious perspective as a gift from my family of origin, and it has shaped my relationship with my family throughout my life. My Christian faith is where I find my self-esteem and identity, but my roles as a husband and father far outweigh any other role in their importance. They make my past make sense and make my future worth living. I see my family as my number one ministry. They represent the best opportunity for me to demonstrate love, grace, forgiveness, and generosity daily. I believe that they are the proving ground for me to learn how to be more like Christ, and that the way I am with my family is a representation of my true and authentic self.

As I reflect on the path my life has taken, family is the common thread that is present in every memory. During those moments when I find myself giving gratitude and thanks for my life's blessings, I often find myself thinking about the members of my tribe who were there for me the most and served as constant sources of inspiration, encouragement, and support. This takes me back to my earliest childhood memories in the Henry Horner projects on the West Side of Chicago.

Most of my memories of that time are a bit sketchy. In fact, my wife and kids roll their eyes when they hear me tell people I'm from the projects, because they know I was still quite the youngster when I left... BUT the few recollections I do have of that time are vivid. I remember the arguments my parents would have and the tears my mother would cry afterwards. I remember when my mother put me on a train to live with my Aunt Millie and Grandma Liz in Lima, Ohio. My family wasn't perfect, but they did their best to live out the words in 1 Timothy 5:8 that talk about the importance of taking care of your relatives, especially those within your own household.

Thanks to a few Polaroid photos, I can see that there were times I spent with my father in Chicago, but I don't remember those times outside of those pictures. I recall going to school, and the fights that would break out. If someone came to your classroom door, balled up their fists, tapped each eye, their nose, and their mouth, and then pointed outside, it meant they wanted to fight you after class. I remember that gangs were a form of identity, and I remember chants of "mighty mighty Blackstones," references to the Black P. Stone/Blackstone Rangers gang. I can still see in my mind's eye the gang fights that would break out in the projects. I recall how we would have to move out of the way when the gangs would run by us on our apartment balcony chasing each other, and how the only thing protecting us from the danger of falling from the high-rise buildings was the chain-link fences that rose up from the landing to the roof.

I have memories of seeing gang activity from the balcony of our fenced residence. I remember watching the "L" trains noisily move along the tracks high above the streets. One of my most vivid memories is of going to the store one day with my brothers and one of us kicking a paper bag that was on the floor as we walked through the grocery store doors. To our surprise, a bunch of food stamps scattered across the floor from the bag, and we excitedly picked up our loot.

I remember a little bit about the schools we went to and the various houses we moved to after leaving the projects. I remember the plastic beads hanging from the living room entry at home, as was the style back in the disco days of the late '60s and early '70s.

Those heated arguments I remembered between my parents would soon lead to their divorce, leaving my mother to raise five children on her own. Ronald is the oldest and has always been a quiet but steady influence in my life. I've always seen him as a competent and capable person who leads by example. He is dependable, and if he gives me his word on something I know he'll always come through. I've never known him to do harm to any person, and my love and respect for him are deeper than I think he realizes. I'll always appreciate how gifted he is as an artist and as an athlete. He almost walked onto a minor-league baseball team without ever having played in high school, but unfortunately didn't make the final cut. I think I initially got my love of sports from him, watching ESPN with him in the early days when it first debuted, and that is something that's easy for us to bond over even to this day.

Maurice (who I mentioned earlier) was next, and I looked up to him a lot and continue to admire him to this day. He was the first of us kids to join the military, and the image of him in uniform is still burned into my mind. Maurice helped me understand the power of images of people who look like us in giving us a sense of belonging. He would later become my motivation to join the military myself; he helped me believe that the U.S. Air Force was a place for me. Today he's still a positive role model and influence in my life, and one of my most valued confidants.

I was the third kid, followed by my brother Bobby. After the entire family relocated to Lima, Ohio, my mother struggled to provide for all of us, and eventually sent me and Bobby to Fort Pierce, Florida, to live with our great-grandmother. In those days, Bobby and I were very competitive and fought and argued a lot. Today he's among my very best friends and I talk with him and Maurice nearly every day. Bobby has grown into a man I deeply respect and admire. We served our military careers together, albeit in different branches and locations. We're constantly sharing insights with each other on topics ranging from world hunger to whatever sporting event was televised the night before. My conversations with him and Maurice get so deep that we refer to them as "podcasts". I think if they were podcasts, the phone would be ringing off the hook from our listeners weighing in on our discussions, especially on those topics about which we are on opposite ends of the spectrum. He has been a wonderful steward of the blessings God has brought into his life and abundantly shares those blessings with everyone privileged enough to be a part of his world.

Cynthia came along as number five, and she always possessed a calm and gentle demeanor. She learned from our mother's example and did the best she could with what she had. I have profound respect for her sense of humility and the kindness I've seen her display to others. Now that she's a mother herself, the success her daughters are experiencing in the world is a wonderful return on the investment of love she poured into them from the beginning. I can always expect the best spirit of hospitality when I visit her. I don't know if we've ever had an argument or disagreement, and there has always been an air of mutual respect between us.

Two other children would join our family later from a relationship that Mom had after the divorce. Their father largely abandoned them as well, so my mother went from raising five children by herself to raising seven. Robert was number six, and my fondest memories of him were when we would go out and do yard work together as our side-hustle to make money as kids. Robert will always have a special place in my heart. He is very practical and down-to-earth. An example of this is when I asked him a question once and he looked at the smartphone in my hand and yelled, "Google it!" He was so right. He has always been the kind of person that people gravitate towards, as he exudes undeniable charisma. I cherish memories of hanging out with him during our childhood and welcome any opportunity to connect with him to this day.

Charlene was last, but certainly not least. Most of her childhood was spent with many of her siblings grown and out of the house. From an academic standpoint, I remember she did better in school than all of us. She is intelligent, resourceful, and determined, someone who can accomplish anything she puts her mind to. She is the sibling who I missed the opportunity to connect with the most when we were kids, due to my entry into the military shortly after my high school graduation. I am proud of the way she persevered through hard times growing up and the work she's put into raising her children and getting her certification as a professional welder.

My mother's approach to raising us continues to serve as an inspiration to me. I will be forever grateful for the sacrifices she made to provide for us despite limited job opportunities, considering she never graduated from high school. She worked hard and constantly kept multiple jobs to make sure we were taken care of. She would later get her G.E.D. in her forties, and I feel privileged that I was able to review her assignments and help her with the work required to reach this huge milestone in her life. If you had met my mother in her later years, you would've observed someone who was quiet and kept to herself. I can tell you, though, that I remember her being very different when I was growing up. She kept five boys and two girls in line and ruled with a rod of iron. She was tiny in stature but mighty in her influence. I also remember that my mother's family was close-knit; she had strong connections with her family and when she turned to them for help, they were there. When I went to live with my aunt and grandmother in Ohio as a young child, Aunt Millie treated me the same way she did her own children. I remember how young my aunt and grandmother were and the things they were trying to do to establish themselves and their careers, but they willingly opened the doors of their homes to yet another mouth to feed.

I grew up fatherless until my early teenage years, when I reconnected with my dad while he was living in Detroit. I harbor no hard feelings toward him today, as God graciously allowed us to reconnect and establish a strong bond in my adult life. For a few years after we reconnected, the five of us who were his biological children would visit him during the summers while we were out of school. The first few times we visited him, I remember how hungry we would get during the day when he was at work. We would scavenge through the pantry, and it seemed like the only thing we could find were jars of peach preserves that we would open and eat. We brought this news back to my mother when we returned home, and I could see the steam pouring through her ears as she realized her children were going hungry under his care. She didn't say much to us about it, but she and my father had a "discussion", and every time we went to visit after that there was always more than enough food to go around. One of the greatest gifts my mother gave her children is that she never spoke harshly about our father throughout our childhood. I never knew whose fault it was that they divorced and never really asked questions about it until my thirties. The unconditional positive regard she showed my father freed me to establish a relationship with him when I began visiting him in my teenage years and has been a great example to me of how love never keeps a record of wrongdoing.

It wasn't until my adult years that I learned that he never paid child support to my mom, forcing her to depend upon government welfare to help put food on the table. Thinking back on this gives me even greater appreciation for the work my mother did and the sacrifices she made to provide for seven kids. I later learned that she got off of welfare once we got older and were able to contribute to help relieve the financial burden she bore alone, and that my father eventually had to repay the government every dime he owed her from the missed child support. To me, that's the way welfare should work. It should be there to assist those like my mother for as long as they have genuine need. After being financially abandoned, my mother depended on government assistance while she needed it and then declined the help and worked whatever job she could when the need was no longer there. Then, the system was compensated by my father when they caught up with him and had him pay back what he rightfully owed. I respect them both for doing what they did, because to the best of my knowledge, my father never balked at paying the government back for the missed child support. Also, I would be remiss if I didn't credit my wonderful stepmother, Gloria, for being my father's "conscience" during this time and holding him accountable to do the right thing. Gloria has always been a source of encouragement and support for me. From the first time we met to this very day, she has been generous with praise about the job my mother did raising us. She is the kind of person I call on when I need a pep talk, words of advice, or to connect with someone who I know will always be truthful with me and not just tell me what I want to hear. Her advice has always been sound, and I consider her part of my inner circle, one of the few who I can be totally transparent with.

My family of origin created the foundation of who I am as a person. Physically, mentally, emotionally, and spiritually, they breathed life into me and served as the initial influence shaping the person I would become. Their inspiration continues to uplift me today. They taught me resilience through challenges, grace through mistakes, and the power of connection through every shared moment. Because of them, I learned to appreciate life's blessings and developed the courage and work ethic to earn whatever I wanted and did not have. As a family, we didn't always get it right, but that's because every family is composed of imperfect people. Most families contain people we can be grateful for, who provide encouragement, support, and inspiration we can use on our life's journey. I will be forever grateful for the role my family played and continue to play to create in me a mindset of constant growth and improvement in my life.

As I reflect on the impact my family has had on shaping who I am, I realize that their love, struggles, and sacrifices are woven into every part of my story. Their influence reminds me that no part of our story is insignificant—it all matters.

Now, I challenge you to consider the role your own family has played in shaping your journey. Whose influence shaped you growing up? What lessons have you learned from their triumphs or struggles? How do these insights shape the person that you are today? Understanding the of who you are and embracing your family's contributions to your story will help you share your story more authentically. Your family is foundational to creating the unique person that you are today.

Chapter 2

Moments:
Kickstarting Personal Growth

"If you want to reach your goals and fulfill your potential, become intentional about personal growth. It will change your life." —Dr. John C. Maxwell

Our life is a series of moments connected by time. Some moments are more memorable and appear to be more impactful than others, but all moments are important in defining who we eventually become. As I think about the catalyst that started me on a journey to personal growth, there's one specific moment that routinely comes to mind. I'll share with you the specifics of that moment, but first, let me set the stage for why personal growth is important.

A mindset bent on personal growth and development is imperative if you're ever going to positively contribute to the life of someone else. Attempting to positively impact others when you haven't developed a mindset based on growth amounts to being on an airplane during a loss of pressure and trying to assist the person next to you without putting your own oxygen mask on first. You must first have the life-giving presence of oxygen flowing through your lungs before you can become an essential part of the crew and help others.

In my natural human state, I would much rather take the path of least resistance and live life as comfortably as I can. I think that even the most motivated and dedicated among us have some measure of this tendency within us. However, 2 Peter 3:18 (KJV) directs the reader to "grow in grace, and in the knowledge of our Lord and Savior Jesus Christ," and I am committed to that growth for any of us, whether we are committed to personal growth as part of our spiritual discipline or have some other motivation, I believe that to move beyond seeking a life of comfort and intentionally and make ourselves uncomfortable so that we grow into our potential, there needs to be someone or something that serves as our primary catalyst. There must be a WHY that is bigger than us. For those who embrace a path of personal growth, they often can pinpoint a singular time or event that caused their shift.

Now, let's get back to the moment that put me on my own path to personal growth. As a young 4th or 5th grader, I had a short career in crime that started when I inadvertently put a candy bar in my coat pocket after my brother wouldn't buy it for me. I didn't realize I had stolen the candy bar until I was halfway home from the store and felt it in my pocket. After seeing how easy it was to get away with theft, I began taking candy on a regular basis. One day I was asked by my mother to clean the attic in our home. Knowing that there was no operational light in the attic, I went to the grocery store to acquire a flashlight and batteries…with no money. The manager of the grocery store let me know that he was aware of what I was doing, and I took off running. As he chased me in his platform shoes (they were in style back in the '70s), I looked back and noticed that the heels had broken off his shoes and he had stopped running.

To this day, I think God pinged my conscience and caused me to stop and turn around and go back to the store, even though I had a clean getaway. Noting my contrition and young age, the store manager called my mother instead of reporting the incident to the police. I experienced a memorable time of "correction" with my mother that still resonates in my mind (and my rear end), such that I never stole anything ever again. As I reflect on that time, I also remember that the pain from the whooping wasn't the only pain I experienced that day. I'll never forget the look of anger, disappointment, and hurt in my mother's eyes as she walked into the store manager's office. After my whooping, I remember going into the bathroom and looking myself in the eyes as the tears still rolled down my face. I made a promise to myself, and later to my mother, that I would never again be the cause of the kind of pain and disappointment I had caused her that day.

Leadership author John C. Maxwell often says that personal growth is the only guarantee we have that tomorrow will be better than today. His statement reminds me of a story I once heard about a five-year-old boy who wanted to go out in the backyard and throw the ball with his dad. The boy repeatedly came into his father's office and asked if they could go out in the backyard to throw a ball. After the boy came in the third time, the dad flipped through a stack of magazines on his desk, pulled one out, thumbed through the pages and found a picture of a globe. He carefully tore the page out of the magazine, cut it up in several pieces, and gave it to his son as a puzzle to put together, with the promise that when he was done, they'd go out and play ball together. Thinking he'd bought himself an eternity because five-year-old boys haven't had geography yet, he went back to work. A few minutes later, the boy returned to his dad's office with the globe put back together correctly. True to his word, the dad closed his computer, put on his shoes, and walked with his boy towards the back yard. Before he opened the door, he looked at his boy and asked, "How did you get that put back together again so quickly?" The boy looked at his dad and said, "On the other side of the page there was a face of a man, and I knew if I could get the man right, the world would be right."

Every time I share that story, the message of that last line becomes more and more powerful. "If I could get the man right, the world would be right." My journey of personal growth helped me to see that if I wanted my world to be better today than it was yesterday, I could only make that happen by being a better person today than I was yesterday. I had to change my "stinking thinking," so I started reading books and became intentional about my growth. I began reading books by authors like Napoleon Hill and W. Clement Stone. I gravitated to titles like *Think and Grow Rich* and *Success Through a Positive Mental Attitude.* I embraced Napoleon Hill's idea in *Think and Grow Rich* that "every adversity has the seed of an equivalent or greater benefit," so that when something in the land of Not Quite Right happened to me, I began to program myself to not think like a victim, but instead to find the possible benefit in that situation. I committed to memory quotes like "Sow a thought and you reap an action; sow an action and you reap a habit; sow a habit and you reap a character; sow a character and you reap a destiny" (Ralph Waldo Emerson). I listened repeatedly to the Personal Power tapes by Anthony Robbins and was mesmerized by the words of author and motivational speaker Zig Ziglar as he stated that "the most important conversation you will have all day is with yourself." I used those words to move my self-talk in a more positive direction, so I could use the power of my mind to lift myself up and not tear myself down.

This season of self-improvement helped me realize that my eventual destiny in life is not based upon what someone else does or doesn't do, but instead is based on my own thoughts. Those thoughts will influence my actions, so ultimately my destiny is in my hands.

I want to dedicate this portion of the book to the person who ignited my commitment to personal growth: my mother, Lillie Mae

Richardson. My mother passed away a few years ago, but I am forever grateful for the role she played in putting me on the path to self-improvement. Promise made…promise kept. The only tears I was ever responsible for after the flashlight incident were tears of joy as she witnessed the many things I achieved.

Often, single mothers are not given the credit they deserve for the job they do raising young men. As I mentioned in the previous chapter, my mother raised seven kids and successfully helped us survive the projects of Chicago in our childhood years prior to our move to Lima, Ohio. For me and my brothers, the power of our mother's influence helped prepare the five of us to serve a total of seventy-five years in the military—two of us served in the Air Force, two in the Army, and one in the Navy—as well as earn nine college degrees between us. For the last ten years of her life, my brothers and I did everything we could to show her our gratitude. We made sure that she never had to pay her own bills, and as her health declined, we moved her into my home and cared for her until her eventual journey to her heavenly home. I can say without a shadow of a doubt that my mother's parenting is the single most important factor that put me on the path to becoming a better man.

As you tell your story, I invite you to share with others the moment(s) that launched you on your own path to becoming a better person. If, for whatever reason, you don't consider yourself to be on that path, I invite you to consider who or what in your life constitutes a "why" big enough to move you in that direction. Make tomorrow better than today by taking personal responsibility to step into tomorrow better than you stepped into today. Identify your "why" and allow it to serve as a catalyst to move you forward. For those of you who do understand your "why" and are already on this journey of personal growth, use your story to help inspire others. When you tell your story, don't just mention the good parts. We need to know the good, the bad, and the ugly. Our failures and shortcomings give us a measure of relatability to others, since failing is common to the human condition. Embrace the key moments in your story, including your failures and the lessons you've learned from them, and share both the failures and the lessons with the world around you. Remember that all your life experiences work together to shape your purpose as you move forward.

Chapter 3

Purpose:
Focus and Direction

"Don't ask what the world needs. Ask what makes you come alive and go do it. Because what the world needs is people who have come alive." — Howard Thurman

Discovering the purpose of our lives is not a singular event. As I reflect on my life, I can see that purpose for me has often been defined by the season of life I find myself in. Ecclesiastes 3:1-8 (KJV) says:

To every thing there is a season, and a time to every purpose under the heaven: A time to be born, and a time to die; a time to plant, and a time to pluck up that which is planted; A time to kill, and a time to heal; a time to break down, and a time to build up; A time to weep, and a time to laugh; a time to mourn, and a time to dance; A time to cast away stones, and a time to gather stones together; a time to embrace, and a time to refrain from embracing; A time to get, and a time to lose; a time to keep, and a time to cast away; A time to rend, and a time to sew; a time to keep silence, and a time to speak; A time to love, and a time to hate; a time of war, and a time of peace.

My understanding of the importance of purpose as an essential element of a life of significance originated from a very personal decision I made when I was sixteen years old—my decision to believe the story my uncle Paul told me about how the purpose of Jesus Christ's death, burial, and resurrection more than 2,000 years ago was to build a bridge between me and God. He helped me understand that if I invited Christ into my life and trusted His finished work on the cross to forgive my sins, I could live the rest of my days as a Christian and fulfill the purpose and plan God had for my existence. When I made this decision, following God as a Christian became the cornerstone of my purpose in life. My life became aligned with King Solomon's words in Ecclesiastes 12:13 (KJV): "Fear God, and keep His commandments: for this is the whole duty of man." Jesus gave further clarification on the priorities of God's commandments when He said in Matthew 22:37-40 (NIV), "'Love the Lord your God with all your heart and with all your soul and with all your mind.' This is the first and greatest commandment. And the second is like it: 'Love your neighbor as yourself.' All the Law and the Prophets hang on these two commandments." My purpose in life was to follow these scriptures.

While being a good Christian is my life's main purpose, the core themes of my life have changed and evolved over time. There was a season in my life that seemed to revolve around my military service. There was a season when raising a family with young children took center stage. There was a season when transitioning out of the military and establishing a post-military career was top-of-mind. The stage I'm in now has to do with helping to add value to the sphere of influence I have and establishing a legacy for my children.

When it comes to gaining true clarity on our life purpose, no matter the season we're in, there are times when it's a struggle. It can feel like we're all over the place with no clear focus or direction. It reminds me of a farmer planting seed but being unsure about what kind of harvest they'll reap. There are times when we know we're planting good seeds, putting our best out in the universe, but there's no harvest, at least not one we can see. It seems like all the seeds we're planting in life are simply blowing away in the wind. Often when we make an investment in something or someone, we want to see immediate results and a return on that investment. Over time, becoming a person of faith has helped me to understand the importance of perseverance in the face of this kind of uncertainty. Think of a farmer. Farmers always reap what they sow, but they reap later than they sow, and at times they reap more or less than they sowed. Some seeds immediately germinate, while some take longer, and other seeds never take root and produce any kind of crop. One thing is for certain: the farmer can only see the results of their hard work paying off after the harvest. Purpose is that way too. It's hard to identify while looking forward, but as we look back over the tapestry of our lives, our purpose is woven into the fabric of our existence with exquisite detail, almost as if our lives have been intelligently designed by someone greater than ourselves. Psalms 23:6 (KJV) says that "goodness and mercy shall follow me all the days of my life." Since goodness and mercy are following us, that means we must look behind us to see the results of their work.

The amazing thing about God's word as recorded in the Bible is that the laws of sowing and reaping work not only for the farmer, but for each of us as well. Isaiah 55:10-11 (NIV) states:

> *As the rain and the snow come down from heaven, and do not return to it without watering the earth and making it bud and so that it yields seed for the sower and bread for the eater, so is my word that goes out from my mouth: it will not return to me empty, but will accomplish what I desire and achieve the purpose for which I sent it.*

When my uncle spoke to me about Jesus, my heart was open and fertile to receive his words, and I fell in love with the Bible and the God of the Bible.

The interesting thing about my Christian conversion was that my family thought it was a phase at first, and my mother did not want me to listen to my uncle (her brother) due to some inconsistencies she perceived in his life between what he said and how he lived. I had trouble in my family because of my decision to become a Christian, and was often accused of letting my uncle brainwash me. It was through these difficult times that I learned how to persevere, and my faith grew stronger each day, laying the foundation for the way my life would unfold in later years.

I'll never forget when my relationship with my family took a turn regarding their acceptance of my faith. One thing my mother often scolded me about was my reluctance to do chores, specifically cleaning the kitchen on my assigned day. With seven children in the house, dishes would pile up quickly if they were not done on schedule. There was no automatic dishwasher in our home. It was all manual labor, and we children represented the labor force. Through my Bible studies, I had learned this:

> *Whatever you do, work at it with all your heart, as working for the Lord, not for human masters, since you know that you will receive an inheritance from the Lord as a reward. It is the Lord Christ you are serving. (Colossians 3:23-24, NIV)*

Internalizing this truth helped me to make serving Christ the focus of my cleaning the kitchen, knowing that it would please Him. My mother was the first to notice this real change in me, seeing that I always left the kitchen spotless on my assigned day, and would even sometimes clean the kitchen on days that were assigned to my siblings. I could sense her becoming more accepting of my decision to spend time going to Bible studies, and I felt an overall increase in the warmness with which she related to me. I realized that if the gospel message was to ever resonate with my family, it would be the result of the gospel I lived, not just the gospel I spoke.

This approach also taught me the value of being responsible for my part and trusting God to do His part. I reflected on 1 Corinthians 3:7, which talks about how one plants and one waters, but only God can give the harvest, and the spirit of that verse came alive to me. I learned that I can only be responsible for my own choices, and I must understand the boundaries that are in place for others to own their choices as well. I learned that God is the ultimate agent of change in my life, as well as in the lives of others.

This season of life helped me develop my entire sense of purpose. I was focused on loving God and serving others. For direction, I asked God daily to order my steps and allow His word to be a "lamp for my feet, a light on my path" (Psalms 119:105, NIV).

When I look back on each of the seasons of my life I've mentioned earlier in this chapter, I can clearly see that His divine purpose for me has unfolded in an orderly way, leading me to precisely where I am today. It all makes sense in hindsight. Some seeds I planted in life came up immediately, allowing me to see the results of my efforts. Some things I did required decades for me to see the results. For example, when I earned my master's degree in aeronautical science early in my military career, it would be decades later that I would use that degree in getting a job. When I earned my master's degree in counseling, I put it to use immediately while still in the military. Through everything, I have been clear on my purpose and my core reason for living. I resolve every day to be an instrument in the hands of God so that His love can flow through me in all that I am and all that I do. This is the singular purpose of my existence.

Perhaps your sense of purpose is not faith-based like mine is. I would encourage you to identify your purpose using whatever matters to you. Some find their sense of importance and direction in their work, in their family, or even in their possessions. Purpose, using the words of author Dr. John C. Maxwell, includes a challenge for each of us to "be a river, not a reservoir." How does your sense of purpose make you better? Does your sense of purpose equip you to contribute to the lives of others? However you define the reason for your existence, I encourage you to allow the treasures that you possess, both internally and externally, to do more than just flow to you, but to flow through you, so that the world around you is made better because you exist.

Chapter 4

Adversity:

Making Course Corrections

"A bend in the road is not the end of the road unless you fail to make the turn." — Dr. John C. Maxwell

One thing I've learned in my journey is that even if your life is moving in a direction you're satisfied with and you have a sense of clarity regarding your overall purpose, there's no promise there will be smooth sailing. As Aristotle Onassis is credited with saying, "We must free ourselves of the hope that the sea will ever rest. We must learn to sail in high winds." John 16:33 (NIV) makes it clear that "in this world you will have trouble." There are times when I've heard very accomplished people talk about their achievements, but neglect to mention the adversity they've had along the way. To achieve maximum impact in sharing our stories with others, we must share the struggles we've had and the specific actions we took to overcome those struggles.

If people who have achieved success were totally honest and transparent, they would tell you that they've built their houses of success with the bricks of failure. Navigating life's troubles or adversities requires agility—the ability to be responsive and adaptive to changing conditions. Agility is the key to thriving despite the moments when life doesn't go the way we thought it would, when we fall flat on our faces and have to deal with failure and disappointment. It is often said that F.A.I.L. stands for **First Attempt In Learning**. Often failure is a gift to those who have the courage to examine their situation and take advantage of the wisdom that is a byproduct of the failure.

However, failure can also paralyze us, rob us of our faith to try again, and keep us shackled by chains of fear. F.E.A.R. has been referred to as **False Evidence Appearing Real**, because failure may create false evidence in our minds that prevents us from moving forward. I've also heard that F.E.A.R. can stand for **F**orget **E**verything **A**nd **R**un. Fear may cause us to lose sight of the wisdom and perspective we could gain from our own experiences in times of difficulty, and also close us off to learning from the experiences of others.

I prefer to think that F.E.A.R. stands for **F**ace **E**verything **A**nd **R**ise. Instead of seeing failure and fear as an excuse to quit, we can use it as motivation to keep going. This view can inspire us to make our stumbling blocks into stepping-stones, to turn our trials into triumphs and our tests into testimonies. When the wheels come off the bus, the way we think will determine whether we gain wisdom that helps us try again, or we use adversity to justify throwing in the towel.

My biggest failures in life were in school. School struggles and spankings (or whoopings as we called them) often went together in my early years. I remember the thing I got in trouble for the most, both at school and at home, was being disrespectful towards my elders. For example, back when I was in junior high—now usually referred to as middle school—I got in trouble several times for making fun of an industrial arts teacher named Mr. Kusmaul and laughing at his "booty chin." (When I shave my beard, you can see God's sense of humor, as my chin looks distinctly similar to the chin I spent so much time making fun of.) Whenever I terrorized Mr. Kusmaul, I would get sent to the front office to get "paddled" for my mischievous ways. Then, after I got home, Mom would continue the corporal punishment. Those days are burned into my memory forever.

I realized that clowning around in school was not conducive to my goal of avoiding pain in my rear end. The discipline I received also eventually helped me to understand that even if I didn't always like their methods, the adults in my life were doing their best to help me grow as a person and they deserved my respect. This lesson was driven home to me so thoroughly that when I was raising my own kids, the number one thing that would get them in trouble with me was when they disrespected their mother or any other adult.

While my behavior at school was important, academic excellence was not heavily emphasized in my family. I remember when it dawned on me during high school that graduating from this level was not the end of the educational road for everyone. I learned that other kids planned to go to college, and that a major reason they worked hard to excel was so they could earn scholarships to continue their education at the next level. To my knowledge, my Aunt Ruby was the only person in our family tree who had completed college. In my family, graduating from high school was the pinnacle of educational achievement, and anything beyond that was a pipe dream and wishful thinking.

Excelling in education was not a priority for me until right before my senior year of high school, when my friends started to talk more about where they planned to apply to college. One memory that still rings clear in my mind is of a school assembly at the end of my junior year, where I saw a senior receive a scholarship to the U.S. Military Academy at West Point. The kid had a 4.0 GPA, and I remember the administrator talking about how all-inclusive the West Point scholarship would be in paying for everything this student would need. I recall thinking how great that was, and how far away I was from ever being able to receive such a deal.

When I built my senior schedule, I elected to take computer math. This was a class that required Algebra 1 and 2 as prerequisites, and I had not taken either. To this day, I still don't know how I was able to get into that class. I took the class and struggled to make it through, earning a D as my final grade. As I neared the end of my senior year, I remember being nervous about whether I had the grades to graduate from high school. I can recall my sense of relief when I found out that yes, I would graduate, because it was not a foregone conclusion in my mind. As graduation loomed closer, I talked with my mother about attending ITT Technical Institute and met with a representative from the school. That conversation derailed quickly when I learned we could not afford for me to attend.

I didn't give up. The technical school path didn't work, but I kept fighting for another path to college. I changed course and looked to sports to get a scholarship. My siblings and I had always enjoyed sports. My mother discouraged us from playing contact sports like football for fear of injuries, but I enjoyed playing basketball at the local playgrounds and at the courts located outside our schools. I vividly remember playing on the outside courts located at the intersection of Hope & Nova Street in Lima, Ohio. While trying to make my own connection between sports and college, I took a road trip with my brother Maurice to Liberty Bible College (Liberty University today) to see if I could talk the basketball coach into giving me a personal tryout, in hopes of getting a scholarship. This was in spite of the fact that I had been cut from my high school basketball team and served as the team manager (water boy) throughout my high school years.

The years I spent as the team manager are among my fondest memories from high school. It was during this time that I learned about the value I could add to others' lives by serving them. I enjoyed getting the rebounds and passing the ball back to the players to help them develop their shots. I also enjoyed the identity associated with being a part of a team. The coach would let me say the pregame prayer before we left the locker room to go play. The only time I received a sports letter in high school was when I was selected to be the manager for the high school all-star team. I still have that letter and plaque to this day.

The drive I had to get into Liberty stemmed not from my arrogance or confidence in myself, but from a deep faith in God I had developed during my teenage years that if He placed in my heart something to do, then He would draw from His vast resources and supply me with the wherewithal to succeed in that endeavor. I had seen His hand of provision so many times growing up, especially in my side hustles of mowing grass, raking leaves, shoveling snow, and washing windows. I remember how I kept my money in an old cigar box in the closet and how it literally would be overflowing with cash. I began to learn through these experiences that wherever He leads, He feeds, and wherever He guides, He provides, and these experiences of trusting God and seeing His provisions helped my faith to grow.

However, the dream of getting into Liberty did not gain traction. The coach said that they had already given out their freshman scholarships and that I would have to pay for the first year and compete for a scholarship the second year. Our family could not afford the cost of that first year. When I reflect on this part of my journey, I'm once again reminded of the impact my family has had on my life. Even though this path to college didn't work out, I still have fond memories of how my brother Maurice encouraged and supported my goal of attending Liberty, and how he jumped in the car with me and made that seven-hour and forty-minute trek at the drop of a hat. The support and encouragement he showed me then have only grown in the way he treats me more than forty years later.

I decided to follow Maurice's lead and enlist in the U.S. Air Force. I battled with whether this was what I was supposed to be doing, as I had other people within my sphere of influence telling me they believed God wanted me to go to Bible college and join the ministry. These people of influence in my life included my pastor at the time, Charles Dupree, and the men at our local church who served as my mentors. However, I knew I needed direction and a sense of purpose for my life, and I believed the Air Force might be the best way to obtain both. I believe God solidified my decision to join the military as the right path for me when, the night before I went to basic training, I led my roommate to receive Christ as his

Savior. The next morning, we parted ways as he headed for the Army. God used this experience to help me understand that my pulpit would not be a traditional, static one, but a global one that would go wherever I would go.

I went to basic training in San Antonio, then transferred to technical training at Keesler Air Force Base in Biloxi, Mississippi. My first assignment after technical training was to K. I. Sawyer Air Force Base in the upper peninsula of Michigan. This assignment introduced me to next-level cold and snow. It was a place where you had to plug your cars up during the winters if you wanted them to start in the morning.

While stationed at K. I. Sawyer AFB, I began attending night classes at Northern Michigan University in Marquette. Then, one day while at work on the base, I stumbled across a pamphlet that someone had left behind on a copier machine that talked about the United States Air Force Academy (USAFA) Preparatory School and Academy. I had never heard of the place, but upon reading the pamphlet, I decided that if I could get in, it would be a great way to get my college education without dragging it out over several years taking night classes. In my ignorance, I assumed it was a college that I could simply sign up for, since it was affiliated with the Air Force. I sent in my application packet and was denied admittance. I tried again and was denied a second time.

At that point, I distinctly remember locking myself into a room for hours at a time studying books about how to improve my ACT and SAT scores. I also remember getting on my knees in the dining room of my very best friends at the time, Chip and Julie Hartin. Chip and Julie and I were inseparable. They were both in the military and Julie and I worked together in the same military unit. I credit their friendship with teaching me everything from how to enjoy the great outdoors to how to show a partner the sort of kindness and support I saw between them as husband and wife. They were the first example I ever witnessed, up close and personal, of what it takes to be in a loving relationship and marriage. While staying at their home one evening, I got on my knees, took out that second rejection letter and held it up, and prayed to God, telling Him that I believed He wanted me at the school, but they kept telling me no. I said, "You are the God of the universe and I know whatever You say goes…so what say You?"

Much to my surprise, the third time I applied, I received a letter of acceptance into the Air Force Academy's Preparatory School. I could go there and sharpen my core academic skills, and then compete for one of the coveted appointments into the Air Force Academy.

Once I got into the Academy's Preparatory School, I immediately began to see where I was strong and where I would need help. My academic record was a problem, along with the fact that it had been three years since I'd finished high school. I spent several semesters on academic probation, but with some extra help from study-skill counselors and my academic instructors, I was able to make it through successfully. I also discovered my strength in military leadership and was selected to be a squadron commander during my Preparatory School tenure. One year later, I competed for and secured my appointment to the U.S. Air Force Academy.

I would soon learn that getting into the Academy was just the beginning of a very difficult journey. The Academy's academic regimen almost proved too much for me to handle. The Prep School was designed to be about 60 percent of what one would experience at the Academy. That added 40 percent was nearly the straw that broke this camel's back. At the conclusion of my first semester, I met an academic review board with a 1.91 GPA. At the conclusion of my second semester, I met another review board with a 1.76 GPA. At the conclusion of my third semester, I met yet another academic review board with three F's and one D. At the time, two F's meant automatic disenrollment, so essentially, my "review" board was an "appeals" board, as administratively I had already been disenrolled. I was number two on the list of those being disenrolled for academics, and number one had decided to resign.

Although I had been elected to be my class vice president, my instructors also rated me lower on my military performance average (MPA), giving me my first sub-3.0 MPA rating since becoming a cadet. The Academy had every reason in the world to deny my appeal and send me home.

I felt embarrassed and ashamed about how I'd performed and feared letting so many people down who had believed in me. I felt like, if I had to leave the Air Force Academy, I would have wasted a golden opportunity to put my life on an elevated path. My biggest fear was that I was about to take a huge step backwards in life.

Once again, many people, including current and former teachers, preparatory school personnel, and current military leaders, came to my aid to recommend my retention. I am so thankful for the people who gave me words of encouragement and "stood in the gap" for me. One person I vividly remember was Captain Kirk Yost, a math instructor whose class I had failed. Captain Yost advocated for me at the appeals board and told the board he didn't care if I failed every *expletive* math course I took as a cadet; they should still find a way to ensure I became a leader in the Air

Force.

The board voted to retain me with a four-to-two tally in my favor. God had shown me once again that despite my humongous failures, He was still on the throne and prayer could still change things.

I was retained on three conditions: 1) I could not keep my selected major, 2) I would not be able to continue as class vice president, and 3) I could not hold any military positions within the cadet leadership structure. I accepted those conditions and proceeded with my cadet career. I realized I had dodged a bullet, and I began to think about what I would have to do differently to succeed. I learned the critical skill of asking for help and realized that I would need to continuously humble myself, check my ego at the door, and ask for support consistently when I needed it. I knew that I had to organize my time differently and use the resources that were available to me that I had been ignoring previously.

I worked very closely with my academic advisor and counselor on course selection. I scheduled some of the tougher courses like Astronautical Engineering and Philosophy during the summertime. My goal was to finish these courses during a time when I didn't have the typical distractions associated with cadet life—sports, military training, and other classes and activities competing for my time. This decision proved to be very beneficial to my GPA, since I got an A in every summer course I took.

Because of my academic challenges, I did not participate in any extracurricular activities during the school year that were not a part of the Academy curriculum. During the summer, however, I completed the aircraft soaring program. I got a sense of satisfaction from this experience as I watched myself struggle with the program, stay steady and continue to learn, then have everything come together for success.

Being at an "Air Force" Academy made this a program that was difficult to ignore. If a cadet had any hopes of actually flying in the Air Force one day, the aircraft soaring program was the first step in training for a future career as an aviator. As for me, I was not aviator-qualified due to my eyesight, so I was interested in the program because it seemed to be the only chance I would ever have to participate in an aviation activity. At the time, you had to have twenty-twenty vision to qualify for pilot training, and my eyesight was 20/400 in both eyes. I had always worn glasses, and being an aviator in the Air Force wasn't something I had ever considered. Unbeknownst to me, a series of events would take place in a few years that would lead to me becoming a navigator and flying as a career aviator.

The soaring program started with flying with an instructor and literally being towed by a gas-powered airplane into the air, connected by a rope. The challenging thing was keeping your flying steady while being towed. We only had a handful of flights before we were supposed to go solo, but I remember how one day it all clicked for me. Seemingly overnight, I went from being very unstable and unsure while being towed behind the plane to being rock-steady.

Prior to the academic review board, I had selected History as my major. As a condition for my retention, the academic review board had all but chosen a Basic Academics major in accordance with my retention plan, but I still took as many history courses as I could to improve my chances of getting my major back someday. Graduating with a major I'd chosen was important to me because it would show that I did more than survive the Academy academically. I wanted to succeed. I wanted to be able to look back on my cadet years and feel proud of my accomplishments. I wanted to know that I had put my mind to something and followed through. I couldn't say that about my high school academic background. I wanted college to be different in that regard.

In my heart I never whole-heartedly accepted the terms laid out for my retention by my academic review board. I felt that the terms limited me and questioned my potential. I believed that if God had enabled someone like me to make it into the Academy, then He surely had what it took to help me succeed. As time passed and my GPA improved, I eventually was able to continue my work as the class vice president. I never relinquished my title or my duties again during my four-year stay at the Academy. This was important to me because this was a position that I'd been elected to; my classmates looked to me and depended on me to serve and to lead in my capacity as vice president. I was determined not to let them down and to fulfill the duties of the office.

Additionally, after showing that I could succeed academically, I was able to restore my history major and eventually graduated with it. Furthermore, I held the highest cadet rank possible as a junior cadet (although not the highest position), commanded Basic Cadet Training during the summer before my senior year (which meant I was the highest-ranking senior cadet in the Basic Cadet Training Program) and was appointed the Cadet Wing Commander for the first semester of my final year—making me the number one-ranked cadet and holder of the highest leadership position in the entire 4,417-person academy. Cadet officers often carry sabers while marching or for other ceremonial reasons. The Cadet Wing Commander is the only cadet who has a gold-tipped saber, and I was the fourth African American in the history of the Air Force Academy to ever hold this cadet rank and position and carry that gold-tipped saber. This selection prompted the Academy Superintendent to obtain a waiver for me to go to flight school (navigator training) after graduation.

All three limitations imposed on me for retention (no leadership positions, no major, no class vice president position) had been overcome to a degree that far surpassed my wildest dreams. This assured me of God's continued favor in my life. But more than anything, the look on my mother's face during my graduation was what made everything I'd gone through worthwhile. She looked so proud, tears flowing from her beautiful brown eyes. I could tell that she felt as much pride in my accomplishments as if they were her own. In a sense, I felt that she had been there with me every step of the way. There would have been no graduation from this prestigious institution without the sacrifices she had made over the years. Looking into her eyes, I knew that my success was her success too. I was the first of her seven children to earn a college degree, and thankfully, not the last. This experience of overcoming obstacles was a wonderful example of God's ability "to do exceedingly abundantly above all that we ask or think, according to the power that works in us" (Ephesians, 3:20, NKJV). With every adversity I faced as a cadet, every bend in my road, I had the courage to make the turn instead of seeing a dead end. I learned to ask for help, and to trust God and the people around me to help me where I was weak. I grew and excelled in areas where I was strong.

My accomplishments as a cadet are things I think about every day as an adult. The memory of those victories fuels me through every challenge in life I've had since then. I'm reminded that no matter what happens, I've seen dark days before, and I have a track record of surviving 100 percent of the challenging days I've faced, because I'm still here. Guess what? The same is true for you!

If a prospective student were to ask me for advice on preparing for college, I would first tell them to start the preparation process early. By this, I mean that they should start ensuring that they develop themselves according to the "whole person" concept well before their senior year. Additionally, I would encourage them to find someone in life who is where they want to be, find out what they did to get there, and see if they can follow a similar path. Then, I would let them know that the most valuable asset they can bring to college is the determination to succeed. They will experience obstacles, but it's their response and reaction to those obstacles that will determine their eventual success or failure. Finally, I would encourage them to get connected to the resources that are at their disposal at the earliest opportunity—to know when to ask for help and not be afraid to do it.

Colleges are typically not in the business of seeing how high they can get their attrition rates. Once you get accepted into a college, it is sometimes harder to get out than it was to get in. To fail out of a college academically, one must intentionally ignore all the well-meaning instructors, counselors, advisors, and organizations that are in place to help one succeed. The sooner new college freshmen learn to build a web of support around themselves, the sooner they will realize that "a threefold cord is not quickly broken" (Ecclesiastes 4:12, KJV). The single thread that tries to exist and succeed on its own is easily snapped. Research suggests that academic and social integration are equally important in succeeding in college. So much emphasis is placed on succeeding academically when connection on the social level is needed as well. Had I failed out of the Academy, in hindsight it would've had more to do with social integration than my ability to pass the academic classes. For me, social integration included time management, learning to relax during exams, and connecting with instructors for extra help outside of the classroom. Many students who struggle incorrectly blame their intellect when the problem may lie in either not knowing about or incorrectly using the resources available to help them succeed.

What I went through to get into college and then succeed in my college experience is a testament to the fact that despite the roadblocks one may find, there is always a way to succeed and reach your educational dreams. Whether you encounter obstacles during the application process or you struggle with the curriculum, personal or interpersonal relationships, or student support services after you're enrolled, there are always people and resources around that are dedicated to the person that refuses to quit. Sometimes these pillars of support are not easy to see. If you're having trouble locating them, contact your advisors for directions. If you still have trouble, incrementally go up the leadership chain asking for help—until you get the leader of the institution, if you must. I guarantee they'll be able to not only connect you to the right person but also correct the issue that necessitated you having to reach out to them in the first place.

Each form of adversity I experienced during my education journey required me to take specific action in order to snatch victory from the jaws of defeat. In the words of English novelist Kingsley Amis, "A bad review may spoil your breakfast, but you shouldn't allow it to spoil your lunch."

In other words, when you encounter adversity, spend a few moments grieving and feeling sorry for yourself, then give yourself a swift kick in the rear, get back on that horse, and ride again.

What challenges have you faced in the past, and how have they shifted the course of your life? In the future, can you use adversity as motivation to redirect your life onto a path that suits you better? Life's failures plant the seeds of success, transforming obstacles into opportunities, challenges into victories, and hardships into powerful stories of resilience and growth. See failure not just for what it is, but for what it can be. It's a seed that has the potential to produce a crop of success, but only if you get back up after falling, take the required action to learn from the wisdom contained therein, and move forward. As you move beyond your failures, always know that none of us can travel our journeys alone. In this next chapter, I'll introduce you to the amazing people who helped me along my own path.

Chapter 5

Connection:
Relationships That Shape Your Life

"Connection is why we're here; it is what gives purpose and meaning to our lives." — Brené Brown

Connecting with others and building positive relationships is key to growing our ability to uplift, support, and encourage others. None of us can do life in a vacuum. We're built for community. Other people are essential to strengthening our sense of purpose and helping us realize our potential. In this chapter, I want to spend some time acknowledging the people outside my family of origin who have done that for me. As Sir Isaac Newton once wrote in a letter to a friend, "If I have seen further than others, it is because I stand on the shoulders of giants," and I want to honor and commemorate the giants in my life for how they influenced me and my growth. There are more than I will mention, so for those who have supported me but don't see your names here, I want you to know that "out of book" does not mean "out of mind" and "out of heart," and that you are part of the "verbal book" I share with others on a continual basis.

Speaking of giants, as a Certified Member of the John Maxwell Leadership Team, I've heard John say many times that "Leadership is influence—nothing more, nothing less." I find it telling that the word 'influence' and the word 'influenza' come from the same Latin root, "influentia" or "influere," meaning "flow" or "to flow in." By our very nature, people are contagious, and we must be careful what we pass on to others with our power of influence. I have always tried to be careful with what I put out into the world because I believe it will come back to me in some way.

As an Air Force navigator, my eyes saw beautiful sights; I visited wonderful places during my military career. But by far, what stands out most from those years in my mind are memories of the people who influenced me and propelled me along the way.

Often, the unsung heroes behind military members' service are our spouses and immediate families. I've often said that the military recruits the members but retains the family, and my wife, Felicia, and our three children, Ryan, Lyndsay, and Nathan, quickly became the "why" behind my continued service.

When we deploy as military members, I believe that it's harder to be the one left behind than it is to be the one leaving. Although we sometimes find ourselves in harm's way during deployments, our primary focus is the mission at hand, while our spouses are left with literally everything else, including all that it takes to be both parents to our children. Felicia rose to all of those challenges, and the way she was the rock of our family was never more evident than when we lost our oldest son, Ryan, in a car accident while I was still in uniform. Her steadfast love and support held our family together. Ever since the day we met over a game of Bible Pictionary in Omaha, Nebraska, Felicia has helped shape my purpose in the military and beyond. You will hear more about my amazing wife and children in the final chapter of this book, when I talk about the importance of legacy—but there was no way I could even think about writing this chapter without introducing you to them and sharing how they are the most important human relationships I have.

My brothers have also played a huge role in shaping my purpose. My brother Bobby is the only other person in my family who has retired from the military—in his case, after more than twenty-five years in the U.S. Army. He and I served in the military mostly during the same time, and although he's younger than me, I look up to him in so many ways as one of my giants. Additionally, as I mentioned earlier, I will always be grateful to my brother Maurice for leading the way into the military for me. He was my inspiration to join. The image of him coming home from basic training in his sharp blue uniform, clean-shaven with a smile on his face and money in his pocket, is still burned into my memory to this day.

My journey to enter the Air Force Academy, which I talked about in the previous chapter, also began because of connections with others that influenced me. The fact that I initially enlisted in the Air Force before entering the Academy is probably the first hint to some of you that my journey to enter a service academy was not a traditional one. For those who are not familiar with the typical path, usually you start by being among the best and brightest of your high school class, then you find a senator or congressperson to nominate you, and then you compete against the best and brightest throughout the country for one of those few coveted slots at the academy. My path to the Air Force Academy began in a very different way.

When I became interested in enlisting in the military, the Air Force was not my first choice. I remember the Army had a huge recruiting campaign going on at the time, and they were advertising their willingness to help students pay for college. I went to the Army recruiter first, but after the person I was talking to had to leave at closing time, I was left to speak to the only other person who stayed late that day—the Air Force recruiter. The Air Force gave me a sense of purpose and direction; it got me "off the streets" and provided an opportunity for me to do something productive with my life. It was a way I could work and be a financial asset to my mother instead of a liability. It was a way I could send money back to her to help her raise the other kids who were still at home. Still, enlisting was a daunting move because a lot of people I associated with at the time thought I should be going in a different direction. I remember that once, even my mother told me that she thought I was "too nice" to go into the military.

When I began the admissions process for the Air Force Academy, the Academy assigned a Liaison Officer to assist me with my application —someone I didn't know personally, who was assigned to monitor applications from a certain region in the state. I began working with this person and soon submitted my first application. Shortly thereafter, as I mentioned earlier, I received a letter saying my application for admission had been denied. When I shared the news with my then-supervisor from my job in the Air Force, Sergeant Dennis Hall, he suggested that to bolster my application packet I should begin competing in Airmen of the Month competitions. These competitions entailed preparing an overview of my career, like a short resume, appearing before an interview panel, and being asked questions relating to everything from U.S. Air Force policies to current local and world events. Typically, a person would be nominated by their supervisor to compete based on their work performance and would compete against the best and brightest within the organization. Sergeant Hall helped me enter these competitions, and soon I began to compete in the Month, Quarter, and Year categories.

At the same time, I was also teaching Sunday school for children at the chapel on the base where I was assigned. One of the other Sunday school teachers had a husband, Captain John Buckley, who was an F-106 "Delta Dart" fighter pilot and Air Force Academy graduate and was on his way back to the Academy to assume a leadership role mentoring cadets.

When he found out that I was trying to get into the Academy, he dismissed my assigned Liaison Officer and took over that role for me. In doing so, he became a personal mentor of mine and helped me make it into the Academy.

As I alluded to earlier, my problems gaining admission were largely caused by the fact that I was an average high school student from an average inner-city high school. This did not lend itself to high SAT and ACT scores. Getting those rejection letters from the Air Force Academy caused me to experience lots of regrets. I began to regret not trying harder in high school. I began to regret my upbringing and my overall lot in life. I began to feel defeated because I knew that I could not go back to the past and change many of the shortcomings the selection process identified. Still, even as I experienced these disappointments, I also remembered the lessons I had learned from the motivational and inspirational books I had read in my life. I remembered that although I couldn't change the past, the future was still undetermined and was largely up to me. I remembered that author Napoleon Hill said, "Whatever the mind of man can conceive and believe, it can achieve." I remembered Bible verses that talked about how what seemed impossible for me was not impossible for an all-powerful and all-knowing God. I remembered that academic excellence was not all that the Academy was looking for. Fortunately, the Academy is a school that focuses on the "whole person" concept, since their goal is to train future military officers. This worked in my favor, since in the year and a half that I had been in the Air Force, I was a Technical School Honor Graduate, an Airman of the Month four out of twelve months, an Airman of the Quarter two out of four quarters, and an Airman of the Year nominee in three different categories, winning it in two of the three. The fact that Captain Buckley also took it upon himself to write a letter of recommendation on my behalf helped give me much-needed leverage.

After my second denial, I added the results from my board competitions along with improved SAT/ACT scores to my third application packet. Finally, I was accepted into the USAFA Preparatory School. Captain Buckley graciously let me borrow his second car to drive from the upper peninsula of Michigan to the Academy in Colorado Springs, since I had to get rid of my car before reporting in. (Personal cars could only be brought to campus by junior and senior cadets.) It meant the world to me that this man, whom I had met just a few months prior, would trust me with his vehicle. Although I was in his car and all four wheels were on the ground, it felt like I floated all the way from Michigan to Colorado.

Captain Buckley's mentorship was crucial to me getting into the Academy. After arriving on campus, I developed a very special relationship with him and his family that proved to be critical to my success as a cadet as well. I immediately had someone at the Academy who would look out for me and be in my corner. I had someplace to go when I needed to get away from the pressures and stress of being a cadet and unwind. Most importantly, I had someone who believed in me and my ability to make it into and through the program. Since he was a Caucasian and I'm African American, he showed me that those who would help me were not confined to a certain race—that good people were everywhere and forgetting that would be detrimental to my future success. Captain Buckley taught me to look beyond color, and to instead look at people through a lens of kindness and acceptance and appreciate each person's individual talents. He taught me that by his example—because that was exactly how he looked at me.

The final giant I want to mention in this chapter is not one person but a family. Each cadet is afforded the opportunity to have a "sponsor" family during their four years. This family provides a home away from home during your time in Colorado Springs. My sponsor family was Wayne and Laura Hopfer, their daughter, Kim, and their son, Kevin. They embraced me as one of their own, even after I filled up their diesel engine car with unleaded fuel. They showed me unconditional love and acceptance and made me feel like family. When I graduated from flight school, neither of my parents could make it to the graduation ceremony to pin on my wings. Mr. Hopfer did those honors. The Hopfers loved and supported me during good times and bad, and over thirty years later, I still stay in touch with them. In a funny coincidence, Kim and I share the same birthday…which happens to be my son Nathan's birthday as well. October is a wonderful month of celebration for us, especially the ninth!

The Hopfer's taught me the importance of family. Observing Mr. Hopfer gave me my first glance at true leadership through service. He cared for each person in his organization and expressed that through his kindness and generosity with his time. I also saw that Mrs. Hopfer was smart and capable and embraced her role as a wife and mother in extraordinary ways. She would later go on to earn her doctorate degree and work as an administrator in higher education. This family will never truly realize the impact they've had on me, or how much of my interaction with my own family is shaped by what I observed in them. They accepted me completely and I consider myself a member of this wonderful family even to this day.

I want to add one more thing before I finish sharing about these giants in my life and how they helped me adapt and succeed. It's important to note that, like Captain Buckley, Sergeant Dennis Hall, Captain Kirk Yost, and the Hopfer family were also not of the same race as me. So often in our culture, we think that the only people who are willing to help us are people who have the same skin color as ours. My experience is that nothing could be further from the truth. These giants "looked like me" in the ways that mattered most. When it came to their humanity and their willingness to offer me their encouragement, help, and support, we all looked the same, and those similarities overwhelmed any external differences between us.

As you reflect on this chapter, take a moment to think about the people who have stayed beside you, lifted you up, and inspired you to keep going. Who are your giants, the ones on whose shoulders you have stood? Who can you reach out to today to share your gratitude, seek guidance, or offer support in return for what they've given you? Where can you look for support in the future? Remember, no one achieves their dreams alone, and recognizing the strength you gain from others is a powerful step in your journey. Your connections are an essential part of what makes your story extraordinary.

Chapter 6

Transformation:
Embracing Teamwork and Community

"The only way to make sense out of change is to plunge into it, move with it and join the dance." — Alan Watts

The transformation of my life has been directly tied to my walk of faith and trust in God. As 2 Corinthians 5:17 (NKJV) says, "if anyone is in Christ, he is a new creation; old things have passed away; behold, all things have become new." I have seen myself move from being a mediocre high school student to graduating from one of our country's most prestigious institutions of higher learning. I have gone from an enlisted personnel specialist to a navigator flying in multimillion-dollar command/control (EC-135 "Looking Glass") and surveillance/reconnaissance aircraft (E-8C "JSTARS") all over the world, amassing about 3,500 flight hours with combat support time over the skies of Kosovo, Iraq, and Afghanistan. I have grown from being a struggling college student to teaching in higher education at the community college, undergraduate, and graduate levels. I have moved from being a program manager/technical lead at a university engineering research center to helping launch a one-of-akind veteran resource center, then becoming a college vice president, and finally starting a leadership training and consulting business. I am filled with gratitude for every opportunity I've been given to continuously reinvent myself.

Life will throw many twists and turns at each of us. For every new challenge that comes our way, we're going to need to stretch and grow and continuously reinvent ourselves to succeed. This kind of adaptability can help string together the seasons of our lives, so that when we look back, everything we've experienced makes sense in hindsight, considering the big picture. When football player Jerry Rice would help his father on construction sites growing up, catching bricks and putting them into place, he probably never thought that the superior hand-eye coordination he was developing would one day contribute to a twenty-year career in the National Football League where he won three Super Bowl titles, a Super Bowl MVP Award, and multiple records for receptions, receiving yards, and touchdowns and was eventually inducted into the Pro Football Hall of Fame. If we're willing to be transformed by our experiences and by the people around us, and to keep reinventing ourselves throughout our lives, we'll keep increasing the value we can bring to the world.

For me, one of the most beautiful aspects of serving in the U.S. Air Force was that for nearly three decades I saw people from all walks of life, who were as diverse as the day is long, working together to create a dominant air and space force that was unified by the goal of keeping our nation free. Our ability to transform from a crowd of individuals into a team created many memories from my career that I cherish and think about often.

One of these memories is of a flight during a combat support mission over the skies of Kosovo. The flight was scheduled as a thirteen-hour mission with one air refueling, meaning going to a "gas station" 26,000 feet in the air that was actually another airplane. Due to the increased combat activity on the ground, that thirteen-hour mission with one air refueling turned into a twenty-one-hour flight with three air refuelings. We had also shown up three hours before launch and then concluded the flight with a standard two-hour debrief—so after everything was said and done, that mission constituted a twenty-six-hour day. I remember that we weren't particularly well-staffed for such a long mission that day, and we had to get creative to make sure we rotated crew members and kept fresh bodies in the seats.

I treasure the memory of that flight because I love recalling how the whole crew responded to this challenge. Even after such a long day, it was difficult for us to sleep that night because we were all so excited about what we had contributed to the flight. We knew that because of our hard work, our willingness to inconvenience ourselves, our flexibility and agility in response to changing conditions, our sacrifice of our own personal comfort, and the unique gifts, talents, and abilities that each of us had brought to the mission, our troops on the ground would be coming home to embrace their families instead of arriving in the underbelly of a plane in flag-draped caskets.

If you were to ask me what I think the secret sauce was, I would say it was the power of unity. During that mission, we weren't individuals;

we were a team dedicated to a singular cause. In an exceptionally trying and difficult time, we remembered our common purpose, and that not only fueled what we did, but also how we did it. We adapted to changing conditions and clung to that unified purpose when the going got tough. After that long flight, we went and got patches made that we wore on our flight suits to commemorate the mission. And even today when I see members of that crew, that mission is always top of mind in our conversation. The night after the mission, as our heads rested on our pillows, we knew that our transformation from a group of individuals into a team powered by a common purpose was what had made the difference that day.

Today, the U.S. is fighting internal battles over the direction of our country and culture that damage our unity and threaten to dilute our purpose. These conflicts are hindering us, as a nation, from transforming into the best version of ourselves. I invite you to join me in holding fast to the purpose stated in our Declaration of Independence—being a nation that provides life, liberty, and the pursuit of happiness to all people. Let's allow that purpose to unite us, rather than throwing in the towel and giving up on the dream of transforming this country from what it was and is to what it can be. With each generation, we can continue to strive, reinvent ourselves, and make each iteration of our nation better than the previous one. Holding on to a common purpose—and allowing it to transform us—will help us find within ourselves the strength we need to "not be weary in well doing," knowing that "in due season we shall reap, if we faint not" (Galatians 6:9, KJV).

Challenging times provide each of us an opportunity to be on the front line, making a difference. Each of us has a role to play to combat racism and social injustice; every one of us can affirm the worth, value, and importance of each person we meet, no matter their background. Somehow, we seem to figure this out a little bit during a crisis, but when life settles down, we often go back to our divisive ways. We must never forget our responsibility to make our world a better place through consistent acts of kindness and civility. We all possess the ability to influence another person. Each of us can be someone else's giant. The worst of times can set the stage for the best of times if we are adaptable enough to reinvent ourselves in response to those challenges. As we grow personally and professionally during times of adversity, we increase our capacity to serve others in ways that can be a game changer for them.

Speaking of times of adversity, during the height of the pandemic and the social unrest at that time, I read an interesting story on social media. The post was about an eighty-seven-yearold man who maintained a positive outlook on life despite the negativity he saw in the headlines of the daily news. He didn't let the headlines shape his entire worldview and lose his faith in the power that each of us has to transform things. Instead, the elderly gentleman tried to create his own headlines that focused on the moments in life that unify us, rather than the ones that divide us, and embraced opportunities to positively impact people within his sphere of influence.

In the spirit of this wise eighty-seven-year-old man, let's elevate our love and care for each other to the center stage of our human experience. Let's make dignity and respect for all of humanity the focus of our daily lives. Despite the negativity that's in the newspapers, on TV, or on social media, let's choose to create our own headlines through positive and uplifting daily actions that create a better today and a brighter tomorrow. Let's all write a new headline today by becoming someone's inspiration. Let's work together to find common purpose and to transform our communities from what they are to what they can be, believing that the best is yet to come.

Below is a poem I wrote many years ago about an imaginary encounter with an ant colony. It speaks of the responsibility and opportunity we have each day to not only transform ourselves, but to help transform others—because interdependence, not independence, should be our rallying cry each day.

TOGETHER

Today I spoke in an unusual way to a very unusual ant.

Outside he worked with all his kind, giving and taking commands.

Get over here, he said to a lonely straggler. Over there, he said to another.

Every day I remind you time and again to help out your sisters and brothers.

Today, the ant said, is a special day, a day when I'll teach you all

How to reach out your hand, help your fellow ant, and not let one another fall.

Every time I think of that small ant's words, I realize our world could run better.

Realizing this truth, whether elderly or youth, how much we could all do...TOGETHER!

Being part of a team or community can transform your life in powerful ways, helping you find support, purpose, and the opportunity to grow alongside others. When you step into a community, you contribute your unique strengths while learning from the talents and perspectives of those around you.

What team or community could you contribute to right now? What passions or skills do you have that could make a difference? If you're not yet connected, where can you start looking to find a group that aligns with your values and goals? Remember, belonging starts with a single step. Are you ready to take it?

Chapter 7

Conclusion:
Impact Leads to Legacy

"The wealthiest place on the planet is just down the road. It is the cemetery. There lie buried companies that were never started, inventions that were never made, bestselling books that were never written, and masterpieces that were never painted. In the cemetery is buried the greatest treasure of untapped potential." — Myles Munroe

Ephesians 2:10 (NLT) tells us, "We are God's masterpiece. He has created us anew in Christ Jesus, so we can do the good things he planned for us long ago." We have a responsibility to be the best stewards we can be of the treasure we are. Each of us is required to lead our lives with integrity as it relates to our story. When I think of the word "integrity," I'm not only referring to the traditional definition of being a person of character or a person of your word. In addition to those things, I also consider integrity to be the ability to hold things together under pressure. Think of an airplane wing. That wing has structural integrity if it can be exposed to the temperatures and stresses associated with flight and help keep the plane safely airborne during a mission. For me, integrity has to do with being made of the right "material" so that whatever my hands find to do, I can be the right person, both inside and out, to succeed. If we are indeed God's masterpiece, as declared in the quote from Ephesians above, there should be no doubt that we're made of the right stuff.

The experiences that made up the fabric of my life continued to create a distinctive tapestry after I graduated from the U.S. Air Force Academy in 1990. In August of that same year, I entered navigator training at Mather Air Force Base in Sacramento. I completed navigator training and, after a six-month stint working in the Air Force ROTC department at

UC Berkeley, went to advanced flight training at Castle Air Force Base in Merced, California. My first operational flying assignment was to Offutt Air Force Base in Omaha, Nebraska, as part of the crew of the EC-135 "Looking Glass" aircraft, a modified Boeing 707 that during the years of the Cold War had flown around-the-clock missions in support of national strategic objectives. Unbeknownst to me, Omaha would also be the place where I would meet my lifelong friend, love, and future mother of my amazing children.

Shortly after I completed my qualification training for the EC-135, I dared to reach beyond the boundaries of a four-year college degree and began pursuing a master's degree. The military encouraged officers to obtain a master's degree to be competitive for future assignments and promotions, and there was an assistance program where the military would cover 75 percent of an officer's tuition. Some of the married men with children in my military unit also encouraged me to finish my master's degree before starting a family. I enrolled in Embry-Riddle Aeronautical University's Master of Science in Aeronautics program, specializing in Aerospace/Aviation Operations. Although Embry-Riddle's main campus was in Daytona Beach, Florida, Offutt AFB had a satellite campus, and I began taking evening classes there.

It was somewhat daunting for me to start the master's program. Classes were challenging after completing a full day's work at the base, which often included flying long missions. Still, I saw other people with similar positions at Offutt completing the program, so I figured I could too. I looked at the experience as one of eating an elephant one bite at a time. Besides, in comparison to the academic rigor of the Air Force Academy, I surmised that very few academic challenges I would ever face would be as grueling.

In May of 1994, I graduated with my master's degree. Although I was a bit disappointed in my 3.57 GPA, it was a far cry from my undergraduate GPA, and that was progress. I saw this as the end of the road for my formal education, but little did I know that life's turns and twists would lead me back to formal education, and that there were still two additional college degrees in my future.

While I'd been in Nebraska studying for the master's degree in aeronautics, I met my future wife over a game of Bible Pictionary. I had been invited by my close friend, Brad Robinson, to attend a going-away party for a guy who was about to leave for a military assignment elsewhere. The party was at the home of the daughter of a local pastor in Omaha and was being put on by the church's youth group.

When it comes to romantic relationships, for most of my life I've been a loner. I did not date much in my younger years. I had always known that I wanted to get married and start a family, but I had also always been very focused on achieving the goals I'd set and left myself very little time to develop a social life. When I first arrived in Omaha, I had tried my luck on the dating scene and had quickly become overwhelmed. As a young professional and a college graduate, I found that I was a rarity, and it didn't take long for me to realize I was in well over my head. I told my friend that I would go to this going-away party with him on one condition— that he would not let me get anyone's phone number, as I literally said to him that "I needed another phone number like I needed a hole in my head." Little did I know that I would meet Felicia Kimes, my bride-to-be and future mother of my children, that very evening.

Felicia and I dated for two years and were engaged for one year. We broke up a few times during our courtship, but always managed to find our way back together. Our wedding was a joyous occasion shared with family and friends, and to this day it still reigns as the best day of my life. I'll never forget how we danced until every guest had left the reception and it was only the two of us and the DJ. Marriage has proven to be a phenomenal experience. My wife has become my best friend and someone who I am privileged to let know every detail of my life. She shares my ups and downs as well as my hopes and dreams. She has helped me to develop a life of intimacy that far outshines the drudgery of a life of isolation. The reality of my relationship with my wife and the wonderful children we have has far exceeded my wildest expectations. Felicia is the most amazing and wonderful person I've ever met.

Our children are absolutely mind-boggling. I continue to be in disbelief that I could have something to do with such amazing people. When they were young, Felicia and I quickly began saving money for their college education. This is something that we felt fortunate to be able to do. Our hope was that this would enable them to start their lives with more of a "leg up" than we had. My dream for my children is that they will maximize the wonderful potential God has given to each of them.

In the early years of my relationship with Felicia, our assignments took us from Offutt AFB in Omaha to Robins AFB in Warner Robins, Georgia, where I would fly the E8-C "JSTARS" aircraft from 1997 to early 2002. Next, shortly after 9/11, we moved to the Pentagon in Washington, DC. While stationed at the Pentagon, I was asked to return to the Air Force Academy as part of a new cadre of leadership to respond to sexual assault and rape allegations plaguing the institution and its cadets. One of the requirements for the job was to be sent to the University of Colorado in Colorado Springs (UCCS) to receive a Master of Arts degree in Counseling and Human Services. I accepted the assignment after only a year at the Pentagon, and our family moved out west to continue our Air Force journey.

In May of 2004, I graduated from UCCS with a 4.0 GPA—the only 4.0 GPA I ever received. This 4.0 was confirmation to me that my academic struggles as an undergraduate at the Air Force Academy were not because I wasn't smart enough, but because I wasn't working smartly in terms of time management and proper study skills, things I had learned over time. The counseling degree was the first time I really felt I received tangible and useful information from a college program that could affect my growth both personally and professionally. I've always believed that success in any endeavor is based upon your ability to deal with and relate to other people. This degree, more than any other, taught me the competencies and skills to do just that. Additionally, during this assignment at the Air Force Academy, I decided that when I retired from the military, I wanted to be a part of higher education administration and perhaps become a college president one day. I loved watching higher education transform other people's lives as it had mine.

We left the Air Force Academy in 2006 and I headed back to Robins AFB in Georgia for another assignment flying the JSTARS aircraft. After three more years on active duty, I retired from military service in 2009.

One thing I've always appreciated about being in the military is the call to be a lifelong learner. At the time I retired, the military was putting the finishing touches on one of the best educational benefits I'd ever heard of. The Post-9/11 GI Bill gave me the option of furthering my own education or passing education benefits along to my wife and/or children if I so desired. However, based upon the timing of my retirement relative to the effective date of the benefit, I was in a situation where I could not pass my benefits to my family and had to either use the benefits myself or lose them. Not ever being one to leave money on the table, I decided to begin searching for Ph.D. programs to apply to.

Initially, the very thought of taking the GRE and interviewing for Ph.D. programs was very daunting. At first I was interested in getting a Ph.D. in Counseling Psychology, but every program I found would require taking classes more than a hundred miles from home. After spending so much time in the military traveling and going on deployments, I didn't want to make that kind of investment of time away from my family, especially to do something that wasn't absolutely required to put food on the table.

Eventually, I reflected on my goal to become a college president one day, conceived during my years of working at the Air Force Academy, and selected the Educational Leadership Ph.D. program (Higher Education track) at Mercer University. I remember being overwhelmed by a spirit of gratitude and thanksgiving to God as I drove the hundred miles between Bonaire and Atlanta, Georgia, to interview for the program, because I never imagined getting a Ph.D. would be possible for me. About two weeks after interviewing with a room full of professors and administrators, I was notified that not only had I achieved a satisfactory score on the GRE, but I was also accepted into the Ph.D. program.

The program followed the cohort model, and my cohort started with about thirty people. Little did I know that only five of us would graduate after the standard three years of study, and I would be the first of the five to complete the journey. Completing a Ph.D. is not easy, especially when you're a forty-something-year-old adult who is married, is working full-time, and has two school-age children. I learned a lot during my time in the program—most importantly, how much I had to depend on the help and support of my fellow cohort members, family, and friends to achieve success, along with trusting in God. Once again, God showed me the amazing things He can do when we surrender our desires, talents, and abilities to Him.

Success, regardless of your chosen field, is never convenient. I have observed that successful people inconvenience themselves from one peak of achievement to another. For a peak to be a peak, there must be a valley on the way to it. Looking back at my experiences, I can see that the times of my greatest growth—whether that growth was academic, professional, spiritual, or in another area of my life—have always been times when I was called upon to stretch myself and reach beyond the comfortable. As an example, going from someone who wasn't sure he would graduate high school to attempting the rigors of a service academy education was certainly one of those stretches. The challenges I described during my cadet years at the Air Force Academy hurt. They hurt mentally and emotionally, and they stretched me spiritually to new heights. Growth experiences are often painful times, but those painful times make the rewards so much sweeter. My successes have always contained failures along the way that became the source of future wisdom and perspective. Success and failure work together, and together they paint a picture of our lives that neither one can paint alone.

I remember there was a particular ten-year period in my career where it seemed like I changed jobs every year. For those who have experienced military service, it is a well-known fact that just because your general career field stays the same, that doesn't necessarily mean your job stays the same. During those ten years, I went from being a line flyer, where my primary job was to mission-plan and fly, to being in leadership positions ranging from flight commander in a training unit to assistant director of flying operations to executive staff. Then I went from being at the Pentagon to being a graduate student, to being a commander, to being executive staff again, etc. Each transition to a different job left me starting at a point of minimal knowledge and expertise, and by embracing the challenge of taking the job, I launched myself to higher heights.

My attitude in approaching the constant job changes was based on the age-old saying "leave things better than you found them." A key element that helped me during each transition was the continuity binder left by my predecessor. In each new position, it became my goal to leave the person who took over for me a more refined and useful continuity binder than I had inherited. My philosophy was that, if my replacement failed in the first six months, then I must own some part of their failure (unless, of course, they did something illegal, immoral, or unethical). If I'd done my job training my replacement, then they should have been set up to survive at least the first six months; after that, it was up to them.

The way the military encourages each airman to increase the width and breadth of their background and experience has created a certain growth mentality within me even as I've navigated the civilian sector. I believe we should all challenge ourselves to be in a constant state of growth, and I don't believe that the learning we do needs to always be confined to the classroom or the workplace. At one point I tried my hand at coaching my son's sports teams and enjoyed the thrill and excitement of those new challenges. I can also see myself possibly taking up a new language or learning to play an instrument sometime in the future. I am a believer in being a life-long learner. I find myself searching and looking for fresh challenges after doing the same thing for a year or so. I think the search for a fresh challenge played a huge role in my desire to seek my Ph.D. This constant quest for change does come with the pitfall of having to start over again and again as the "new guy," and with each new job having to climb a mountain of knowledge, experience, and expertise. However, these challenges are easier to handle if I keep my focus on serving others with my leadership skills and removing barriers that are keeping those around me from realizing their full professional and personal potential.

Now that I've finished telling you my story so far, I want to reflect on the legacy I'll leave behind. Today, our family resides in Bonaire, Georgia, a few miles from Robins AFB, my last posting before I retired from the Air Force after twenty-six and a half years in uniform (which included four years as an Air Force Academy Cadet and twenty-two and a half years of active duty). As I mentioned earlier in this book, after retirement from the military, I worked at Mercer University Engineering Research Center; taught college as an adjunct instructor at the technical college, undergraduate, and graduate levels; was part of the initial leadership team for the Georgia Veterans Education Career Transition Resource (VECTR) Center; and became the Vice President of Student Affairs at Valencia College in Orlando. I currently have an educational and leadership consulting business, Axis Leadership, LLC, and am a Certified Member of the John Maxwell Leadership Team. My company does leadership training and project management consulting for a variety of clients in the Middle Georgia area.

My wife Felicia has a very successful career as a Victim Advocate Coordinator for the Houston County District Attorney's Office, has two associate degrees, and completed her bachelor's degree in criminal justice from Columbus State University in 2024. We recently celebrated our twenty-ninth wedding anniversary and look forward to many more wonderful years together. On September 29, 2023, Felicia was the recipient of the prestigious Houston County Bar Association Liberty Bell Award for community service. This is the highest recognition from the Bar Association for someone who is not a lawyer. I, along with Lyndsay and Nate, was extremely proud to cheer for her as she received this award. Lyndsay told Felicia that it was great to be "on the other side" cheering her on after all the times Felicia had been there cheering for her throughout her life, words that brought Felicia to tears. That sentiment applies to the whole family. It was a wonderful time of validation for Felicia and a wonderful recognition of all the great things she does for us, for her employer, and for our community.

Our oldest son, Ryan, was two years old when I met Felicia; he was her son from a prior relationship. I embraced him as my own and together we raised him until his tragic accident in 2009, when he became our angel above. Ryan had a heart of service and was in the final stages of processing to become a member of the U.S. Border Patrol. He was the ultimate big brother, even to kids who weren't a part of our family, and especially to kids with special needs. I'll always be grateful to him for many reasons, but especially for all he taught me about being a parent. Whenever Felicia and I would get in a disagreement, he could be heard saying "Man, go to the woman" and encouraging me to take the first step in making amends. He is loved and adored by many to this day, even years after his accident, because he was accepting of all and was a model of what it meant to love unconditionally.

Lyndsay is our only girl and was a model child growing up. There's no such thing as a perfect kid, but she was about as close as you can get. She loved reading and excelled in school. She graduated from Columbus State University with both a bachelor's and a master's degree and is a classically trained opera singer. She got her love of music from her musically inclined and gifted mother and used it to enter the world of pageantry, where she held multiple titles in the Miss America Organization, including Miss Warner Robins, Miss Columbus, Miss Music City, and fourth runner-up for Miss Georgia. She also taught middle-school chorus, fulfilling a childhood dream of hers. She is the perfect blend of personality between me and Felicia, yet she's her own uniquely strong, intelligent, and capable person. She is a wonderful connector of people, a great organizer, and an amazing thought-partner. During the initial years of my consulting business, I was fortunate to have her serve as the Operations Manager for Axis Leadership, LLC.

Nathan is our youngest child, and he was born on my thirty-seventh birthday—an incredible present. He joined a host of October birthdays on my side of the family, including two of my brothers and one of my sisters. Nathan is a very kind and compassionate person who values the friends that are a part of his inner circle. Like his mother and sister, he is musically inclined. He has perfect pitch and is an incredible musician who plays multiple instruments, including keyboards and the trombone. His first love is mathematics, though, and he's currently a junior at Kennesaw State University in Georgia, where he is combining his love of music and math in his music production major. Nathan also works alongside me in my leadership consulting business as a Junior Accountant.

I am incredibly proud of my family, and my hope is that Axis Leadership will be a part of the legacy I pass on to my children for generations to come.

I believe we have all been given a predetermined number of days on this earth. I strive to live an inspired life each day and realize my full potential in every way. The Bible instructs each of us to press on toward our goals and "take hold of that for which Christ Jesus took hold of [us]" (Philippians 3:12, NIV) and to "run with endurance the race God has set before us" (Hebrews 12:1, NLT). For most of my life I was a collector of awards, degrees, and achievements. The more I live, the more apparent it is to me that all the success I've achieved means nothing if I don't use it to add value to others' lives and help them connect to their full potential.

I realize that I have been given a story, and it's up to me to be the best steward of that story so that it brings value to the people my life is privileged to touch. Living with an eternal focus and with the perspective that the most important reward I can receive is to hear "well done, thou good and faithful servant" (Matthew 25:21, KJV) at the end of my days has inspired me to live for God first and others second, knowing that if I live with God's priorities in mind that my needs will be taken care of by Him. The church I attend, Southside Baptist Church in Warner Robins, Georgia, has a mission statement that says, "We love God, love people, and love the world on the journey to life change." I think this mission statement is a great one for a church, especially when you keep in mind that the true spirit of a church is its congregation—the people who fill the building, not the bricks and mortar that comprise the building. This great church mission statement is an even better personal mission statement, and I would love to see how our world would be transformed if all people made this statement the reality of their lives.

I challenge each of you reading to do that. I look forward to one day hearing your story about your life of impact and how you've shared your experiences to inspire others. There's no doubt in my mind that someone reading this book has a story so compelling that it will someday be the focus of a song, a book, or even a movie. Never underestimate the power of your experiences to uplift someone else. Sometimes the redeeming value of the adversity we experience is found in how it equips us to help someone else go through tough times. I've always believed that unless you are the ruler of the universe, you cannot categorically say whether something is good or bad. We can say that something hurt us or made us happy, but not everything that hurts us harms us. Only time will tell whether something that was painful at the time was actually a blessing in disguise. A trip to the dentist may be painful, but over the long haul, going through that pain could spare us even greater discomfort in the future.

I want to invite you to see your unique and individual story as a gift of great value. At times, it may be challenging to recognize the value in certain chapters of our stories, but just because we can't see it in the moment doesn't mean it isn't there. Your life was meant to have an impact. The little drummer boy played his drum for the baby Jesus in a way that only he could, and similarly, each of our lives has a unique melody that needs to be heard by others. There is no doubt in my mind that just as the baby Jesus smiled at the little drummer boy, God will smile on us as we use our stories to impact this world and to bless and encourage others in ways that are unique to each of us.

Respond to the clarion call. Become a fellow laborer with me. Don't live and have your story be untold, the song of your life unsung. Don't bury the light of what you've been given under a bushel. Let your story shine bright from the mountaintop and be proclaimed with excitement and joy to all willing to listen. I guarantee there's somebody on this earth who needs the encouragement and inspiration that can only come from you and your unique life adventure.

The motto of my company, Axis Leadership, LLC, is "Better People, Better World." We believe that the best way to make our world better is to do so one person at a time. I believe the stories of our lives each communicate a special and unique message from God. Thus, it is my hope that sharing your story using the principles outlined in this book will create individual ripples, moving from one person to the next, that will eventually combine to create a giant wave of positive change in our world.

From this day forward, I encourage you to embrace the power of your story and allow it to impact the world around you. Play your drum for Him like the little drummer boy did. Sing your song. Do your dance. Write your story. Use Braille, sign language, dance, music, poetry, art, cartoons, musical instruments, acting…whatever you like, but don't leave this world without sharing with us all the wonderful treasure that is you. I wish you all my best on your journey.

God Bless!

The End

Joseph C. Richardson

www.ingramcontent.com/pod-product-compliance
Lightning Source LLC
Chambersburg PA
CBHW060355050426
42449CB00011B/2994